JESUS & THE
HIP-HOP
PROPHETS

SPIRITUAL INSIGHTS FROM
LAURYN HILL & TUPAC SHAKUR

ALEX GEE & JOHN TETER

InterVarsity Press
Downers Grove, Illinois

InterVarsity Press
P.O. Box 1400, Downers Grove, IL 60515-1426
World Wide Web: www.ivpress.com
E-mail: mail@ivpress.com

©2003 by Alex Gee and John Teter

InterVarsity Press® is the book-publishing division of InterVarsity Christian Fellowship/ USA®, a student movement active on campus at hundreds of universities, colleges and schools of nursing in the United States of America, and a member movement of the International Fellowship of Evangelical Students. For information about local and regional activities, write Public Relations Dept., InterVarsity Christian Fellowship/USA, 6400 Schroeder Rd., P.O. Box 7895, Madison, WI 53707-7895, or visit the IVCF website at <www.ivcf.org>.

All Scripture quotations, unless otherwise indicated, are taken from the Holy Bible, New International Version®. NIV®. Copyright ©1973, 1978, 1984 by International Bible Society. Used by permission of Zondervan Publishing House. All rights reserved.

"Can't Take My Eyes Off of You" words and music by Bob Crewe and Bob Gaudio. ©1967 (renewed 1995) EMI Longitude Music and Seasons Four Music. All rights reserved. International copyright secured. Used by permission.

"Every Ghetto Every City" © 1998 Sony/ATV Tunes LLC, Obverse Creation Music and Scanian Music. All rights on behalf of Sony/ATV Tunes and Obverse Creation Music, administered by Sony/ATV Music Publishing. All rights reserved. Used by permission.

"Doo-Wop (That Thing)" © 1998 Sony/ATV Tunes LLC and Obverse Creation Music. All rights administered by Sony/ATV Music Publishing. All rights reserved. Used by permission.

Cover design: Rick Franklin

Cover image: Veer

ISBN 0-8308-3234-3

Printed in the United States of America ∞

Library of Congress Cataloging-in-Publication Data

Gee, Alex, 1963-
    Jesus & the hip-hop prophets: spiritual insights from Lauryn Hill and Tupac Shakur / Alex Gee and John Teter.
        p. cm.
    ISBN 0-8308-3234-3 (pbk.: alk. paper)
    1. Spiritual life—Christianity. 2. Hip-hop—Religious aspects—Christianity. 3. Hill, Lauryn. 4. Shakur, Tupac, 1971- I. Teter, John, 1970- II. Title.
    BV4501.3.G44 2003
    261.5'78—dc22

                                                                    20030316147

P	13	12	11	10	9	8	7	6	5	4	3	2	1
Y	12	11	10	09	08	07	06	05	04	03			

CONTENTS

INTRO: *Follow the Beats* 7

TRACK 1: *Dear Mama* 15

TRACK 2: *Can't Take My Eyes Off of You* 29

TRACK 3: *Every Ghetto, Every City.* 41

TRACK 4: *That Thang* 53

TRACK 5: *Brenda's Got a Baby.* 64

TRACK 6: *Life Goes On.* 77

TRACK 7: *Changes* 94

OUTRO: *'Bout It, 'Bout It* 105

SHOUT OUTS 111

ABOUT THE AUTHORS 114

Tupac, Lauryn and Jesus?

Yes.

Makaveli, L-Boogie and the Son of God?

Sure.

Prophets?

Not exactly Elijah or Isaiah. But prophets nonetheless.

What are prophets?

Who are prophets?

People who deliver an appropriate word for a given situation.

The connections run deeper than you think.

It all depends on what you hear.

A HIP-HOP HOMECOMING

I was walking around the University of Southern California the week of the big football game against UCLA. There was a homecoming rally, but I was on my way home. Then I began to hear some beats. I didn't know a concert was going on. I was curious, so I followed the beats. A stage was set up in the middle of campus, a DJ was scratching, the crowd was pumping their fists. I could hear rapping in the distance. I had to get closer to check it out.

It turned out to be Mac-10. He was flowing for the crowd and putting on a good show. I was enjoying the scene.

I began walking around the back of the crowd to look for some of my friends. Someone looked familiar to me. I had to do a double take. It looked like Trugoy from De La Soul. I got fired up. I had been a De La Soul fan for ten years. And here he was just chillin' on my college campus. I went up to him and said whazzup. He gave me love and we began talking. He was way cool. We talked about education, east and west coast rap, the new emerging styles, the spirituality of college students, Jesus and life. It was a great conversation. After a half-hour, we shook hands and he told me he had to get ready to perform. De La Soul was headlining the homecoming concert. He disappeared. I didn't see him again until later that night when he was moving the crowd.

I sure am glad I followed the beats that night. I didn't know what was on the other end. I just put together that something was up. I had no idea I would get to spend an hour with a hero from my youth. The beats hooked me up.

JESUS AND THE BEATS

Jesus doesn't have weak beats. When he drops a beat or freestyles, our hearts hit heights we never knew existed. Jesus wants to be seen and he wants to be heard. And he wants to invite us into his inner circle.

The biographies of Jesus in the Bible include a story about three astrologers. They probably weren't as shady as Miss Cleo, but they were astrologers nonetheless. Still, God spoke to them. They walked all night through the desert because the stars told them God's Son had been born into the world. They were the first ones to figure out what God was up to, because God wanted them on the inside. God could have communicated with them any way—could have hollered on their cell, dropped an e-mail or hit them on their two-way. But these three saw the stars God had placed for them. They did their mathematical homework and figured out God's plan on their own.

These astrologers had no formal religious background. They didn't feel comfortable at church. They knew what religious people thought about palm readers. They knew people talked trash about them. And they talked trash about others. They were not "religious" people at all. But their faith still serves as an example for all of us today. You would think the religious people would be in the front row for the birth of God's Son. But it was the astrologers, not the stuffy religious folk, who were first to give Jesus props and show him love. The religious people were too busy being religious. They missed God—and still thought they were more spiritual than everyone else.

There are some important lessons to learn from the astrologers about how spiritual growth works. It's not where you are from; it's where you're at. Your religious background takes a big backseat to your religious future. Spiritual growth is not just for the religious but for everyone who is looking for something more in life. If you never went to church and don't know much about the Bible, you should expect God's love to begin crashing into your life. God is self-revealing to the spiritually curious.

Just as God did with the astrologers when Jesus was born, God puts clues in our lives today. Just as the beats led John to Trugoy, the clues will lead us to God. Our heart might begin to beat heavier. Our palms might begin to sweat. Our eyes might strain as we are in God's brilliant presence. And when we find him, our soul will melt when we see his beauty and we realize that the hard journey has been worth it. As we know him more intimately, the script will be flipped. We will begin to realize that while we were pursuing God, all the time God was pursuing us. We will begin to realize just how deep God's love for us goes. It goes way back.

ABOUT US

We live in the real world. We aren't professionals dissecting hip-hop lyrics from an ivory tower. We are spiritual leaders serving hurting people in our communities. Alex is a black man from Madison, Wisconsin. (Alex's personal experiences are marked *AG.*) John is a biracial Korean-white man from Los Angeles, California. (John's personal experiences are

marked *JT.*) We have experienced real problems in life,
and we have seen the power of God to bring hope
and healing to any situation. We know the people we
love look to hip-hop for strength, direction and
comfort. That is why we write. We are fans of the
music. We like Tupac. We like Lauryn. In fact, John
went to concerts to catch Public Enemy, Big Daddy
Kane, Slick Rick and Third Base. We are fans.

We believe our entire generation is being led into
deeper God-knowledge through the music. We just
have to listen, understand and appreciate the heart of
the beats.

We think the hip-hop community has been hated on
too long. People are always in their business. It is easy
to be a critic. But the hip-hop community possesses
unmatched strength and potential. They are a gifted
and courageous people. And we believe God will use
that. Remember, it's not where you're from. It is where
you're going, and most important, where you finish.
The haters don't see that hip-hop leaders are being
raised up for spiritual purposes as a chosen
generation.

The following pages contain our experience of God
through the music of Lauryn and Tupac. We are not

trying to cram Christianity down anyone's throat. We've been around that block. We hated it. Instead we share how the music touches us and draws us closer to God. We invite you into our own thoughts of the music and share with you our own stories of how God has hooked us up.

Our only challenge to you is that you listen to your own soul. Our world today moves fast. We get into patterns. Some are good. Some are bad. But few help us connect with the real needs of our soul. Yet when we slow down and truly listen, we begin to create space for God in our soul.

The astrologers followed the stars and found themselves at the foot of God's crib. As you listen to Tupac, Lauryn and your soul, where will you find yourself?

Listen to the beats.

Follow them.

FOR CENTURIES THE BIBLE HAS BEEN telling us how God is a loving Father who wants only what is best for us.

We have been told that God will protect us,
guide us,
forgive us and,
no matter what, always be with us.

The Bible depicts God as having power, deserving respect and always looking for wayward but much-loved children.

What a wonderful story!

But what good is a wonderful story if the audience doesn't connect with it?

What good is it if it can't be understood?

It is like receiving a computer attachment in a program your computer doesn't have.

It just ain't happenin'.

Many of us have heard the right story . . . but in the wrong language.

What we need is a new program to launch the computer attachment. What we need is a new perspective to understand just how phenomenal this story is. We are all tired of gibberish we can't understand.

▼

God is love!

God loved the world enough to sacrifice the Son for our good.

Love is unselfish.

Love never fails.

Love doesn't keep score.

Love doesn't promote itself.

Love doesn't walk out on you.

Love doesn't leave you to figure out life all on your own.

Love doesn't support you financially just because the courts have mandated it.

Love doesn't miss birthdays . . . graduations . . . weddings . . . or entire childhoods.

When I think about God's kind of love, no man comes to mind.

This doesn't make men bad. I'm a man.

The fact remains, however, that although the love-phrases above describe God, they don't describe a father . . . not to me.

The epitome of love that was unconditional,
Unselfish,
Undying,
Unending,

Was embodied by a woman, not a man, for me.

The epitome of love and commitment is a mother.

Specifically, a single mother who struggled and put her own children's needs and dreams above her own.

A woman who would swallow her own pride and go on welfare and/or work two and three jobs just so that

her family could:
Stay warm and
Fed and
Clothed and
In school and
Oblivious to the fact that times were hard—real hard.

I suspect that this is the case for many people.

I know that this is the case for me.

Our mothers have made us the people we are today.

▼

The Bible gives us images to help us understand God's
relationship with us. For example, Hosea compared
God to a jilted lover who was willing to stoop to self-
humiliation by purchasing his own wife's love from her
pimp (Hosea 3:2). Jesus described God as a shepherd
who would leave ninety-nine sheep to find one lost
one. David, in a psalm, compared God to a hen that
hides her chicks under her wings. And Isaiah referred
to God as a mother. A nursing mother with her child
in her arms.

What image could be more tender, more vulnerable?

What is more natural, heartwarming, beautiful than the loving picture of a mother feeding her child from her own breasts?

This is the epitome of nurture,
Care,
Commitment,
Protection,
Affection,
Affirmation,
Family.

This is God's self-description to Isaiah the prophet:

> *But Zion said, "The LORD has forsaken me,*
> *the Lord has forgotten me."*
>
> *"Can a mother forget the baby at her breast*
> *and have no compassion on the child she has borne?*
> *Though she may forget,*
> *I will not forget you!*
> *See, I have engraved you on the palms of my hands."*
> *(Isaiah 49:14-16)*

And this is how God chooses to reveal himself to you.

▼

I am the father of a healthy six-year-old, Lexi, who was born three and a half months prematurely. She was hospitalized for the first sixteen weeks of her life. Birth had been a major battle for her, and she weighed in at only one pound eight ounces for her fight against sickness. Her health was dependent on her ability to digest breast milk and on my wife Jackie's ability to produce it. Jackie hadn't gone full term with the pregnancy, so the doctors weren't sure that she could produce milk.

A mother's body is stimulated to begin producing milk when she holds her child in her arms or hears the hungry cry of her newborn. We could not hold our child, because she was sentenced to an incubator twenty-four hours a day. And we couldn't hear her cry, because she had tubes in her nose and throat twenty-four hours a day.

The hospital had formula, but it would not be as good for Lexi as milk produced by the woman whose body had carried her. Jackie's milk would be a gourmet meal, genetically prepared with this special baby in mind.

My sister told us that a mother of a premature baby can sometimes be stimulated to produce milk by looking at a photo of her newborn. The nurses encouraged Jackie to try this method. They instructed Jackie to look at photos of Lexi while pumping milk.

To our surprise, it worked. Jackie was able to supply milk for Lexi for six whole months.

So a nursing mother can be stimulated to produce milk by merely seeing her child, or
Hearing the cry of her child or
Simply holding her child.

In fact, a nursing mother *must* feed her child or her breasts become swollen and painful. Breastfeeding brings relief to both mother and child.

The nursing mother's own body is a constant reminder that she has a child.

Through Isaiah, God is saying, "I will never forget you, never neglect you.

"Can a nursing mother who sees her child . . . hears the crying . . . feels the baby in her arms . . . still forget about and neglect that baby?

"Doesn't her own body tell her that it's time to feed the child?

"Doesn't she feel pain when she ignores the baby's feeding schedule?

"Yet," God says,

"Even if this is possible with a nursing mother, it is never possible with me!

"Not now!

"Not ever!"

The picture of God in Isaiah 49 is a gentle, nursing mother and not a proud, pacing father handing out cigars in the waiting room.

Maybe the image of mother is just as sacred as the image of father.

Maybe the image of God as a father is needed to convey certain things to us about God's power and authority.

But maybe the image of God as a mother is needed to convey things about God's nature and nurture and love. Pictures of God that we often miss.

Maybe our eternal Creator, in divine wisdom, realized that we would need a father *and* mother.

God is our all in all.

▼

I have listened to Tupac's lyrics over and over again.

You always was committed

A poor single mother on welfare,
*   tell me how ya did it*

There's no way I can pay you back

But the plan is to show you that I understand

You are appreciated . . .

Now ain't nobody tell us it was fair

No love from my daddy cause the coward
*   wasn't there. . . .*

I hung around with the Thugs, and
*   even though they sold drugs*

They showed a young brother love

I moved out and started really hangin

I needed money of my own so I started slangin

I ain't guilty cause even though I sell rocks

It feels good puttin money in your mailbox

I love payin rent when the rent's due

I hope ya got the diamond necklace that I sent to you

Cause when I was low you was there for me

And never left me alone because you cared for me

And I could see you comin home after work late

You're in the kitchen tryin to fix us a hot plate . . .

. . . And even though I act craaazy

I gotta thank the Lord that you made me

There are no words that can express how I feel

You never kept a secret, always stayed real

And I appreciate how you raised me

And all the extra love that you gave me

I wish I could take the pain away

*If you can make it through the night
    there's a brighter day*

Everything will be alright if ya hold on

It's a struggle every day, gotta roll on

And there's no way I can pay you back

But my plan is to show you that I understand

You are appreciated

▼

I love the way Tupac describes his mother:

She is strong.

She loves unconditionally.

She never gave up on him.

She inspired him and helped him to focus.

She was dependable.

His craziness never dissuaded her from loving him, and she embodied love and commitment.

At times she was blamed for his hardships.

Yet she was the one who worked all day and then put hot food on the table.

She disciplined him.

But it was in love.

He could never repay her for all she had done.

His desire is to show her that he understands all that was done for him.

And that he appreciates it.

Think about the words of Tupac's song. He is

serenading someone. It's apparent that he didn't always understand or appreciate his mother. He was often too angry or too crazy to see all that she had done for him. But as an adult he realizes she was in his corner all along.

Tupac says he was looking for a daddy but couldn't find one. He ran with gangs because they showed a young brother some love.

This pursuit of love cost Tupac a lot.

This pursuit of love is still costing many of our young men and women their lives.

I can understand . . . true love is worth pursuing.

But gangs don't provide real love.

And sex without respect and relationship isn't real love.

True love is not only worthy of being pursued—it is actively pursuing each of us this very moment.

True love pursues!

Here is the secret of receiving God's pursuing love: Get caught!

Remember being a kid and playing the game where the boys would chase the girls and if we caught them we could kiss them and vice versa? If I really liked a girl, I would purposely trip myself and fall so she could catch me and kiss me.

Trip yourself . . .

Stop running and get caught!

God is not asking you to be the pursuer.

God is not asking you to understand everything.

God is not asking you to become a zombie and sell flowers at the airport.

God is not asking you to change your political affiliation.

God is not asking you to change the way you dress.

God is not asking you to dump your friends.

God is asking you to stop running away . . .

And merely asking you to give him the chance to show you love.

How, you ask?

By just telling God that you are tired of looking for love in all the wrong places and that you want something that is real and long-lasting.

Tell God that you believe but still need help with unbelief.

And remember: Your prayers, your faith, your songs, your tears, your groans and your crying are all "photos" that are always before our nursing God, reminding him of our needs.

God remembers us.

God sustains, feeds and nurtures us like a gentle, caring nursing mother.

Like Tupac, we can never pay our "mama" back. But our plan should be to show God we understand.

And as with Tupac, the one we blamed for all of our troubles is actually the one who protected us from the harsher realities of life.

Just tell God that you can't repay what Jesus has done—but you understand.

▼

AS WE WALKED ONTO THE DANCE FLOOR our hearts were soaring. This was one of the greatest days of our lives. It was our wedding day! Ours. This was the moment we would tell our children about. This was our NBA Finals, Academy Awards and Christmas morning all rolled into one.

It may sound like a movie, but Becky and I really did fall in love on our first date. It sure wasn't my Polo cologne or my c-walk or my Long Beach shake. That first night was magical. We really enjoyed talking to each other; we hit it off and had mad chemistry. We felt like we were somehow made for each other. And from that day forth we knew we wanted to spend the rest of our lives together.

At our wedding celebration, when we hit the floor for our first dance, everything went Matrix and slowed way down. We had joked about wanting to throw down some cardboard and break dance. (Our Korean and Japanese relatives probably wouldn't have appreciated that at all.) The moment was surreal. We were in a room filled with the people we loved most in the world, but they might as well have been strangers. Nothing else really mattered. As we danced, we whispered and chatted. I don't remember a word. But I will never forget two things. I will always treasure that look on Becky's face. She was so happy. Her eyes were dancing.

And I will always remember our song:

> *You're just too good to be true*
> *Can't take my eyes off of you*
> *You be like heaven to touch*
> *I want to hold you so much*
> *At long last love has arrived*
> *And I thank God I'm alive*
> *You're just too good to be true*
> *Can't take my eyes off of you.*

For our first song people might have expected Frank Sinatra or Natalie Cole, but we wanted Lauryn's song to be our song. We saw Lauryn Hill perform in Los Angeles while we were dating. At her concert I made my move and we had our first kiss. I didn't want our first kiss to be at Denny's or some whack party. Lauryn Hill and her music had been a running theme in our relationship, and we thought that song captured our experience.

The first dance at my wedding was a great victory for me. I had always felt a little nervous about getting married. There were all of the normal insecurities. Would I ever get married? Were my looks good enough? Was I too short? Would I marry someone beautiful? Would I have to settle for someone I didn't really love? But I also carried around a heavier burden.

I grew up fearing that I would be left alone, just as when my father suddenly died in a plane crash. I therefore protected myself and didn't let people get too close. Before I became a Christian, I hid my fears of commitment and getting hurt by hanging with the fellas. After deciding to follow Jesus, I stayed safe in the name of religion. In reality, the common denominator in both situations was my keeping everyone on the outside. But then God ushered Becky into my life. And God's healing. I learned how to trust again. I learned how to know by faith that God would take care of me. I had been afraid that marriage meant I might be abandoned again. But that night I wasn't afraid. I no longer lived in fear. In Becky love had finally arrived and God's healing had taken me to new places.

Today Becky and I have been married for three years. In the big picture, we are young and just starting out. But we have already been through much drama together. We lost a parent to cancer. My mom fell and broke her hip. We have moved twice. We try and juggle big workloads. We are beginning to think about children of our own. We are no longer on the dance floor in a tuxedo and a wedding dress. We are no longer the center of attention. We are now just plain old John and Becky. But the song plays on. Our relationship grows into new dimensions. She's still too good to be true.

We were made for relationships. With each other. And also with God. It is God who created love. The apostle John, one of Jesus' best friends, wrote in the Bible that God is love. All of the passion, commitment, tenderness, forgiveness, joy and delight that make up love flow freely inside God. Humans have blood that runs through their veins. Love flows through God's essence. God is love.

One of the central images in the Bible is the marriage of God and God's people. The people of faith are called to be Jesus' bride. God promised in the Old Testament to one day come to earth and win the hand of the bride. Here is the promise:

> *"For your Maker is your husband—*
> *the LORD Almighty is his name—*
> *the Holy One of Israel is your Redeemer;*
> *he is called the God of all the earth.*
> *The LORD will call you back*
> *as if you were a wife deserted and distressed*
> *in spirit—*
> *a wife who married young,*
> *only to be rejected," says your God.*
> *"For a brief moment I abandoned you,*
> *but with deep compassion I will bring you back.*
> *In a surge of anger*
> *I hid my face from you for a moment,*
> *but with everlasting kindness*
> *I will have compassion on you,"*
> *says the LORD your Redeemer. (Isaiah 54:5-8)*

Jesus was the fulfillment of that promise and taught us what it means that our relationship to him is to be a spiritual marriage. He urged us to be prepared for the day of our great wedding celebration. He promised that he is a loving and patient bridegroom and we don't have to fear anything. He will never leave us, ignore us, get tired of us, talk trash about us or divorce us. He calls us to be loyal to him and forsake all other lovers. And he promised that one day, after we die, we will be the center of attention at a great wedding celebration in heaven, the kingdom of God.

The best things on earth are mirrors of realities in heaven. Faith has its rewards!

God's wedding celebration will be the best banquet ever. It will not be held at a restaurant, a yacht or even an earthly mansion. It will be at God's house. And Jesus promises that we ain't seen nothing yet! God's house makes the mansions on MTV *Cribs* look like cardboard boxes on Skid Row. That is where our great wedding celebration will be. It is way too good to be true.

But God is not just ushering us as his most honored guests into eternity. All that stuff is easy for God, and it will be a reality tomorrow. Today God offers us himself. We were created to enjoy and love God. This is not just for heaven. It can be our experience today.

We all need more love in our lives. We all need better

relationships. When we drink in God's love, our thirst is quenched. When we drink in God's love, destructive patterns are shattered. When we drink in God's love, we become the people we were meant to be. When we drink in God's love, we become satisfied. When God is our center, all other things fall into place. We were created for love.

▼

God loves us so much!

Not because we're good.
Not because we deserve it.
Not because we've earned it.

But because God loves the way it feels to love.

Years ago, God entered the world as a little baby in order to demonstrate love for us. An angel gave this child a special name, Immanuel, which means God is with us.

Not God is against us.
Not God is gonna get us.
Not God is angry at us.

Not God has forgotten about us.

But God is with us.
Or God supports us.
Or God believes in us.
Or God thinks the world of us.
Or better yet, God's got our back.

Immanuel.
God is with us.

This is why God came to earth. God wanted to convey a very urgent message to us:

"I got your back, baby!"

It's hard to tell someone that you're there for them when you're a million miles away—in heaven. So God came to earth to show solidarity with our hurts and pains. God came to do more than just observe. God came to get involved.

Think about Jesus for a minute.

He has always been around his father,
And they have always been around the Spirit.

Always.

All three have always been love.

Always.

But then the Son came to Earth and everything changed.

Who was he going to kick it with now?

He had always been in a Holy Huddle: Father, Son and Holy Ghost!

Since the beginning, he had been a part of this holy family.

But now he was on the earth.

He must've been real homesick so far from that kind of love and that kind of family.

He loved the Holy Huddle.

But since huddling was his specialty,
Why not start a Holy Huddle on earth?

Why not use the same passion of huddling in heaven . . . and huddle on earth?

And guess what? Jesus is just as committed to huddling with us as he is with the Father.

I think that this is actually why he came to earth.

To be committed to huddling with his created beings just as he had with the other Two.

So . . . God is with us.

And what is he whispering in the Huddle?

> *"Whoever touches you touches the apple of [my] eye!"*
> *(Zechariah 2:8)*

Wow.

The Hebrew word for apple means "pupil of the eye."

Hmmmmm.

The eye is so sensitive that it has its own protective covering, the eyelid. Even when you're not thinking about it or trying to, the lid protects the eye against injury or discomfort. This is built in at birth.

And nothing will intrude and touch God's eye. Not without a reaction!

God is saying, "It is easier for someone to sneak up on me when I'm not looking and poke their finger in my eye and get away with it, than for someone to hurt you—and I not feel it!

"That's why I can't take my eyes off you.

You're the sensitive part of my eyes.

You're in my head . . . I can't take my eyes off you.

It's impossible.

You're in me.

"That's why you're like heaven to touch . . . You are protected.

Because you're my reward.

That's why I want to hold you so much,

Because of what it does for you . . .

Because of what it does for me . . .

Because of what it does for us.

"Pretty baby, I found you.

You didn't find me.

You couldn't.

"It is I who found you, how is it that you think you can lose me?

You can't lose me!

I'm everywhere.

And so is my love for you.

"So now that I've found you, stay.

And let me love you.

Always.

Always.
Always.

"Oh pretty baby,
You're too good to be true."

> *How great is the love the Father*
>   *has lavished on us,*
>   *that we should be called*
>   *children of God. (1 John 3:1)*

GOD IS ALL ABOUT THE BIG PICTURE. God is often called the master potter. And the greatest divine sculpture is our very lives. Each of our lives is a wonderful work in progress. We may wish that the artist would work faster, or use different tools, or adopt a different style. But God has a plan for you and for me.

God the potter knows the big picture of what our lives will become. God sees twenty years in the future and knows what we will need to get there. In great love for us, the Artist uses immeasurable talent to turn our greatest sufferings and defeats into our greatest victories. The Artist knows what bumps and blemishes are needed to be worked out to reach the end goal. God is committed to the final product and will mold every experience we go through for our good. This is the central thrust of "Every Ghetto, Every City."

Lauryn Hill did not become Lauryn Hill overnight. She did not go worldwide in a moment. She became who she is today because of the people who were placed in her life. She became the strong woman she is today because of the pain she has gone through. And whatever city in the world she is in, she knows that she got there because of New Jersey. Our past is a vital part of our future.

> *Move the patch from my Lees*
> *to the tongue of my shoe*
>
> *'Member Frelng-Huysen used to have*
> *the bomb leather*
>
> *Back when Doug Fresh and*
> *Slick Rick were together*
>
> *Looking at the crew, we thought*
> *we'd all live forever*
>
> *You know it's hot, don't forget*
> *what you've got*
>
> *Looking back*
>
> *Lookin' back, lookin' back, lookin' back*

We all come from unique beginnings. Not one of us had a choice about what family we would be born into, where in the world we would be born, when we would be born or what gender or race we would be.

These things were the Creator's choice.

Lauryn Hill thinks about her development during her time in New Jersey. She looks back and remembers the cool people she kicked it with. She remembers the dreams she and her friends had. She looks back and remembers how her friends, like Slick Rick and Biz Markee, became world-class rap stars. She doesn't forget her roots. She doesn't forget her family. And she doesn't forget the people who believed in her. She is who she is because of her past.

Unfortunately, many of us believe that our past disqualifies us from the future God has ahead of us. We think that because we acted wildly we have fouled out of the game. We think that since we are tainted goods, we can no longer be brought into the inner circle with God and his divine purposes. That is not true.

God does not see us like that. God sees not only our past and our present but who we will become in twenty years. God has given us our past and put dreams in our heart for a very special purpose. No one has the past and the passions we carry. What we have been through, our greatest struggles, may become our greatest gifts to this world. God sees you. God sees me. And who we will become.

▼

I was sitting next to my friend Todd in our third-grade art class. We had just studied watercolors the previous week, and now Mrs. Gilbert, the teacher, announced that we would be working with clay. Clay? Well, okay, that looks just like brown Play-Doh to me, I thought to myself. Not being much of an artist, I did the only thing I knew to do: I simply put one hand on top of the other and began to roll the lump of clay beneath my palms. When asked what I was making, I chuckled and commented that I wasn't sure; it would either be a little snake or a huge cigar. After I rolled awhile, I looked over at my friend Todd to offer him a puff of my clay cigar. I was stunned to see that Todd had sculpted an animal. It looked as nice as a figurine I'd seen on my grandmother's dresser.

I said to him, "Wow, that's real cool. How did you make that little puppy?"

"Oh, it's easy," he said. "I slam the clay up and down on the table, looking at the lump each time in order to see if anything appears. When something appears to me out of the lump, I peel away the clay I don't need and out jumps what I'm making. It's simple!"

Although I never saw anything in my lump of clay
except snakes and cigars, my conversation with Todd
that day helps me to better understand what God is
saying to us.

We are created and called with great contemplation
and care.

Jeremiah was a young prophet who lived a long, long
time ago. He was stressing because God wanted his
life to be full of incredible stuff and he was insecure
because of age and experience. He told God that he
couldn't do it.

God told Jeremiah that his birth was not a mistake,
nor was it an afterthought: "Before I placed you inside
your mother's womb, I, like a potter, saw exactly what
I wanted to create you to be. Your abilities and
qualifications have nothing to do with this.

"You can do it!

"You can be what I am asking you to be because I am
living inside of you.

"And from time to time I'll remind you that you're
bigger than you believe . . .

"And from time to time I'll remind you that your life has purpose . . ."

One day the great Potter felt inspired.

He walked to his pottery wheel and took a seat.

You could tell from the curled-up smile on his lip that he was up to something pretty special. Now he chuckled as he grabbed a lump of clay.

The pedal began to move and the wheel slowly began to spin.

"What'll it be?" asked all the angels. They all knew that look—when the Potter was not to be disturbed, when he was in artistic flow.

And slowly,
Methodically,
He began to give shape to a new image.

Well, not really new, it had been within the Potter's head and heart.

It was just new to the world.

Brand new!

A Heaven original.

But I must admit . . .

I didn't realize that the Potter put so much time and energy into forming us.

I just thought people had babies that eventually grew up.

I didn't know that God, the Potter, sits at a wheel and creates each of us,
With care,
With caution,
With joy,
With authority,
With a unique blueprint.

▼

God told Jeremiah that he was trippin' over his lack of experience. God knew all about Jeremiah—good and bad.

There are no accidents in God's plan. The Potter knows exactly what he is doing when calling us to a task. In a more modern language, God is saying,

"Look, Jeremy.

"Before you were even in your mother's womb,
Before your father was old enough to carry life
in his loins,
Even before the beginning of time,
I had great thoughts of you, your life and our
purposes together.

"I didn't want you in the Garden of Eden;
I chose Adam.
I didn't need you to lead my children out of Egypt; I
assigned that task to Moses.
I didn't need you to succeed King Saul on the throne;
I picked David for that purpose.

"However, I have strategically placed you in this
moment and timed this moment for you.

"I have waited an eternity to become friends with you
and to call you to my purposes.

"Now you are telling me no because you don't feel
qualified?!

"Don't you get it!? The only reason you are who you
are is that I'm calling you to be a part of my plan."

We need to flip the script. God doesn't fit into our
lives; our lives fit into God's plans.

That is why we look back. God has placed the secret of our future in the foundation of our past.

▼

They say that Monday morning makes the best quarterbacks. Hindsight is always 20-20. That is true for our spiritual lives as well. As we look back on our lives, God's purpose becomes clearer and clearer. The potter is always at work. As we see what he is forming us into, our greatest questions will be answered and our greatest pains will be healed.

I feel like I have learned the secret of life itself. God is the artist, and I am his work. God controls the wheel, he uses the tools, he owns the clay, and he never lies. If God says he is going to make something, he will. I believe that as with Jeremiah, God has seen what I will become. And he has already put those foundations into my life.

I am currently thirty-three years old, and my life is full of hope and confidence in God's love. As I serve college students in Long Beach and Compton, I understand not only why God has me here but how he got me here. As I look back, I do see the Creator's care, caution, authority and attention to detail in all facets of my life. As I look back I understand why:

Why was I born Korean-White? Why was Alex born Black?

Why was I born in Los Angeles? Why was Alex born in Chicago?

Why did I love to write as a kid? Why did Alex love astronomy?

Why did my father die in a plane accident when I was eleven? Why was Alex's dad not around?

Why did I grow up with a hip-hop DJ as my best friend in high school? Why did Alex have musical gifts?

Why did I launch myself recklessly into the party scene? Why did Alex embrace God's call early on?

Why did God answer my desperate prayer and miraculously save me moments before I would have drowned in the Pacific Ocean? Why did God reveal himself to Alex miraculously at age eleven?

And why did God have me meet Alex Gee, one person out of twenty thousand people at a conference in 1996?

Why did God put Becky Sato into my life? Why did God put Jackie Malone in Alex's life?

There are no accidents with the Potter.

I see the work of the potter, and the sculpture my life is becoming, and I am thrilled. As I look back, I can't wait for what comes ahead.

What do you see when you look back?

For Lauryn, each day she is reminded of her destiny.

Destinies don't just happen.

Destinies are designed and accepted.

Lauryn saw that each experience
in New Jersey,
good or bad,
prepared her for her destiny.

Do you see the Painter?

Do you see the Potter?

Do you see the God of Jeremiah?

Do you see the God who has seen you?

Do you see the God who knows who and what you will become?

Do you see how God is using artistic tools in your life?

Do you see the God who can turn your greatest defeats into victories?

Look back.

You will see your future.

Trust God.

Don't try to jump off the potter's wheel.

The Potter's hand is sure.

God's plans are better for you than you think.

> *I praise you because I am fearfully and wonderfully*
> > *made;*
> > *your works are wonderful,*
> > *I know that full well. (Psalm 139:14)*

THE PHONE RANG AT MIDNIGHT. It had to be important. Becky picked it up and began counseling and comforting Maria. Something wild had gone down and she was freaking out.

Crisis was nothing new on our street. We lived in an apartment in South Central Los Angeles. Three active gangs were on our block. The ghetto bird buzzed us almost every other night. We even had the bird shine in on our bedroom window. It turned out that the 5-0 came over to ask us questions about one of our neighbors who struggled with some ghetto tendencies.

Freddy was one of our neighbors. He was an eighteen-year-old banger who had two strikes against him. One more felony and he would be in prison for twenty-five years. But when you are desperate, you do desperate things. He owed a drug dealer some big jack, so he jacked one of our neighbors for their television. While he was climbing out of the window, someone saw him and put in the call. Minutes later, the police chopper was whirling above our street in full force. Freddy was hiding in the bushes, waiting for the opening to get home.

At that moment Maria got home from her night class at the community college. The helicopter startled her, so she rushed toward her door. But someone called out her name.

"Maria, hey, over here."

She whipped around, looked into the darkness, saw nothing and kept on moving.

"Maria, hey, over here. It's me, Freddy."

"Who is that? Where are you?"

"It's me, Freddy, from the Bible study." (Maria is a beautiful woman and Freddy wanted to get with her. She had become a follower of Jesus through our neighborhood Bible study, so he had attended one night to get to know her better.)

"What are you doing in my mom's bushes?"

"I am kind of hiding out from the police. They are after me right now."

"What? The chopper is looking for you? You better get home right now. I am going in the house."

"Hey, before you do, I have a quick question for you."

"What, Freddy?"

"Did John or Becky tell you that I think you're really cute? I was wondering if we could go to Starbucks together sometime."

Maria didn't know what to say. She couldn't believe that was happening.

"Freddy, I'm going in my house. You better go home!"

She went inside, and Freddy somehow managed to cut through the backyards of South Central, television in hand, and make it back to his crib.

As Becky told me about Maria's eventful night in the hood, Lauryn Hill's words rang in my head:

> *Girls you know you better watch out*
>
> *Some guys, some guys are only about*
>
> *That thing, that thing, that thing . . .*

Yes, some guys are only about that thang. And yes, some girls are only about that thang. Even with the

ghetto bird in hot pursuit and twenty-five years of
prison hanging in the balance, my man Freddy made
it a point to get his mac on to see if he could hook
something up with Maria. That thang, indeed.

▼

*It's been three weeks since you've been looking
    for your friend*

The one you let hit it and never called you again

*'Member when he told you he was 'bout the
    Benjamins*

*You act like you ain't hear him then gave him a little
    trim*

To begin, how you think you really gon' pretend

Like you wasn't down then you called him again

*Plus when you give it up so easy you ain't even fooling
    him*

If you did it then, then you probably f*** again

Talking out your neck sayin' you're a Christian

A Muslim sleeping with the gin

Now that was the sin that did Jezebel in

Who you gon' tell when the repercussions spin

Showing off your a** 'cause you're thinking it's a trend

The second verse is dedicated to the men

*More concerned with his rims and his Timbs
    than his women*

Him and his men come in the club like hooligans

*Don't care who they offend popping yang
    like you got yen*

*Let's not pretend, they wanna pack pistol
    by they waist men*

*Crystal by the case men, still in they mother's
    basement*

The pretty face men claiming that they did a bid men

Need to take care of their three and four kids men

They facing a court case when the child's support late

*Money taking, heart breaking now you wonder why
    women hate men*

*The sneaky silent men the punk domestic violence
    men*

▼

Men and women pursue that thang for different
reasons. Some want physical intimacy. Some want
power. Some want the image. Others the rush. Many
of us have been pursuing it so long it has become who
we are. We are in the scene so deep, we can't imagine
living any other way. Lauryn is asking us a scary

question in this song. She is playing the role of prophet in calling cultural assumptions into question. The question is whether or not this is the most fulfilling way to live. Will that thang really make us happy?

As I think about what direction things are going, it reminds me of the cycle that the cartoon character Wile E. Coyote seems eternally caught in. We all have a little Wile E. inside of us, and that thang is the Road Runner.

We hear the "beep-beep" and we are off and running.

It doesn't matter what we are doing. When we hear the beep-beep we begin our hot pursuit.

We try and present our image.

We put on our thang face to impress.

We play the games, make the promises and do what it takes to get that thang.

There is something deep inside our soul that tells us we will find something that will heal the broken parts of our life. So we look for the filling of our soul.

But it never comes through for us. It always lets us down. Even when we catch it.

All the energy of the Wile E. Coyote syndrome of buying Acme rockets and setting traps comes into our life through our look, our car, our image. We will buy an Escalade on dubs but live in our mama's basement.

Somehow we left hungrier than when we started.

But then we hear the beep-beep again and we are off and running. But the Road Runner goes off the cliff and we have nowhere to go but down.

Ssshhhhhhhh . . .

Pooof! And up we go with the cloud of dust.

Such is our plight as we pursue that thang. It's hard to catch. So we think maybe our sex isn't good enough. Maybe we should be freakier or roll harder, then we will get "it."

Lauryn's advice is that if we want to win, we better get right within. She is in good company. That is also Jesus' advice.

In John's Gospel, chapter 8, Jesus runs into someone who is caught up in "that thang."

At dawn he appeared again in the temple courts, where all the people gathered around him, and he sat down to teach them. The teachers of the law and the Pharisees brought in a woman caught in adultery. They made her stand before the group and said to Jesus, "Teacher, this woman was caught in the act of adultery. In the Law Moses commanded us to stone such women. Now what do you say?" They were using this question as a trap, in order to have a basis for accusing him.

But Jesus bent down and started to write on the ground with his finger. When they kept on questioning him, he straightened up and said to them, "If any one of you is without sin, let him be the first to throw a stone at her." Again he stooped down and wrote on the ground.

At this, those who heard began to go away one at a time, the older ones first, until only Jesus was left, with the woman still standing there. Jesus straightened up and asked her, "Woman, where are they? Has no one condemned you?"

"No one, sir," she said.

"Then neither do I condemn you," Jesus declared. "Go now and leave your life of sin." (John 8:2-11)

The pursuit of sex has robbed this woman of her human dignity. In that morning meeting with Jesus, she finds herself in major crisis. Her life has fallen apart, and she's cast at Jesus' feet. What will he say? Will he blast her for not keeping her pants on? Will he go the authority route and throw down in public?

Jesus' reaction is unexpected. I bet the people at the religious center of the day expected Jesus to whip out his critical eye. But instead of condemnation, Jesus shows compassion. He doesn't deliver his morality lecture. He knows this woman's life is falling apart. He knows her soul is worn from all of the empty sex, broken promises and stolen dignity.

Jesus never blasts the person who wants to become spiritually whole. Jesus gives back the person's dignity. And his words are the offer of hope and healing.

We can all learn from what went down that early morning. When Jesus gets involved, our sexual past, no matter how dark, how painful or how current, does not disqualify us from the future God sets before us. When Jesus breaks into the most vulnerable parts of our life, like our sexuality, his goal is not to shackle us with guilt. His desire for you and me is that we be liberated by faith. Faith is having a second chance with our sexuality. Faith is the wondrous discovery that there are better things in this world than that thang.

Faith is not about just denying yourself. It is about listening to your soul and making the wise spiritual decisions that will bring you the most happiness.

Fifty years ago, C. S. Lewis, a British author and close friend of J. R. R. Tolkien, wrote about why our souls so often settle. He understood the cycle of that thang that Lauryn Hill describes. Lewis said that when we see the Lord on our big day of judgment, he will surprise us. He isn't going to say that we were unreachable because we were too strong in our passions and desires. Instead, he will tell us that our passions were too weak. He'll scratch his head and wonder why we fooled around with sex, ambition and dead presidents when an authentic friendship with God, and all the benefits of being in his crew, is offered. It is like turning down an all-expense-paid, world-class yacht vacation to the Caribbean because we don't understand what is really being offered. So we just stay in the hood and throw mud at each other all day. We don't understand the nature of rewards, so we settle. We are way too easily pleased.

It is ludicrous to choose to keep playing with dirt in the ghetto because we don't know what it means to cruise to Jamaica on a yacht. We choose to play with mud because we have never seen a yacht. We choose to listen to the screams and noise of the streets instead of the DJ on the yacht's top deck. We settle for jumping through a fire hydrant instead of snorkeling in clear tropical waters. Because we don't understand we choose Flamin' Hot Chee-tos over steak and lobster. Life in the hood over Jamaican vacations is no way to live. Yet we often choose "that thang" because we don't know God has incredible plans for our life. If we listen to our soul, we know that we are meant for much greater purposes than chasing "that thang." The great news of Jesus has a holiday at the sea waiting for you in your sexuality. But you need to drop the mud. That is what real faith is all about.

> *"No good thing does [God] withhold*
> *from those whose walk is blameless" (Psalm 84:11).*

I hear Brenda's got a baby

Well, Brenda's barely got a brain

A d*** shame

Tha girl can hardly spell her name

*(That's not her problem,
that's up ta Brenda's family)*

*Well let me show ya how it affects
tha whole community*

*Now Brenda never really knew her mom
and her dad was a junky*

Went in debt to his arms, it's sad

Cause I bet Brenda doesn't even know

*Just cause your in tha ghetto doesn't mean ya
can't grow*

But oh, that's a thought, my own revelation

Do whatever it takes ta resist tha temptation

Brenda got herself a boyfriend

*Her boyfriend was her cousin,
now let's watch tha joy end*

*She tried to hide her pregnancy
from her family*

*Who didn't really care to see
or give a d*** if she*

Went out and had a church of kids

*As long as when tha check came
they got first dibs*

Now Brenda's belly is gettin bigger

*But no one seems ta notice any
change in her figure.*

TUPAC SHAKUR

▼

Brenda lives in an invisible prison.

A secret hell.

No one seems to be able to see
What has happened to her,
What is happening to her,
And what is going to happen to her.

No one except her warden, who is her sexually abusive
cousin.

Now Brenda's got a baby!

Umm umm umm! What a shame.

Babies having babies.

Umm umm umm! Don't she know better than that?

What was she thinking?

Did she think?

But Brenda's got bigger problems than the baby . . .

And so does society.

The sex that created the baby in Brenda's adolescent womb was her feeble and immature attempt to make her own way.

Brenda was being destroyed before she ever had a chance to live.

Those who should've protected her were too busy living their own lives and regaining their youth.

They left her in the care of her own cousin, who told her he'd protect her and make her feel special and pretty . . .

And she got pregnant.

She had the baby alone on the cold tile floor of the bathroom. The same place she conceived it.

And now Brenda's got a baby!

(We're not any better than that scum that molested her, 'cause we didn't care to protect her and we didn't care enough to notice that she was even pregnant.)

How did this young innocent and unsuspecting thing get here?

Allow me to show you . . .

THE INVASION:
ENTRANCE OF THE ABUSER

Shhhhh!

Step step step

Tippy-toe . . . tippy-toe . . . tippy-toe.

Shhhhh!

The doorknob slowly turns . . .

c-l-i-c-k

c—r—e—a—k—

The door opens very slowly and deliberately.

And he slips inside the door into the darkness of this child's room.

This isn't just a door to Brenda's room
But a door to Brenda's innocence,
A door to Brenda's dreams,
A door to Brenda's very soul.
A door to Brenda's childhood—the prelude to her adulthood.

He didn't knock,
He wasn't invited.

To this twelve-year-old mind, this was too much to bear,
To this twelve-year-old body, this was torture,
To this twelve-year-old soul, this was a curse.
To this twelve-year-old dreamer, this was a lifelong nightmare.
And to this twelve-year-old girl, this was premature exposure to womanhood.

"Shhh! If you tell anyone, you'll die!" he threatened in a whisper.

"When will the morning come?" she asks.

"When will this pain end?" she wonders.

"When will someone hear, feel or see what is happening to me?" she moans.

When will her dawn come?

And just like that . . . her innocence is gone.
And just like that . . . her childhood is gone.
And just like that . . . her molester is too . . .

Until tomorrow night.

Where is the sunrise?

And now Brenda's got a baby!

And what's almost as painful as living with the secret of the father is living without his presence.

And just like that . . . her baby's daddy is gone.

▼

I have hope today for people like Brenda, her baby, her abusers and the people who ignored her as she went through her stuff alone. Because she is not alone. Crazy things happen, but we don't go through it alone. True, no one noticed her figure growing, or the

baby she had just thrown into a trash can. But there is
one who cares. There is one who heals.

▼

I used to never believe that God talked to humans. I
figured he wrote the Bible and that was it. I couldn't
picture him rapping with us like a phone conversation.
In fact, when I heard people say "God told me," I
would think they were insane. But in the spring of
1992, after having serious battles with my faith, I was
about to experience something that blew my mind.

I was enjoying fresh power from God in my life. I
wasn't walking on water or picking up cars. (Though
that would have been tight.) Instead God's power was
fixing my broken life. No headlines, just healing. I
stopped fighting with my mom. I was doing better in
school. I stopped abusing alcohol and drugs, and
driving around faded. I was learning to not see
women as objects. I was connecting more with my
true purpose in life. I felt healthier physically,
emotionally and, most important, spiritually. I felt
more alive.

As I learned to pray in that first year, I sought God with great passion. That's when he broke in and spoke to my heart. I had never heard him speak to me before, but then he captivated my heart and spoke to my soul. He proved to me he was real. It was a trip. I had never had a spiritual experience like this before. His one word suddenly described my whole previous nine months. His one word to me somehow defined my whole life. His one word to me gave me a new power to live my life by.

That morning in prayer, I asked God one question.

"God, how much do you love me?"

Immediately I heard in my soul a still-small voice:

"John, read Ezekiel 16:6-8."

I didn't know if Ezekiel was even a book in the Bible. If it was, did it have sixteen chapters? But I had faith and opened my Bible to see if God was speaking to me.

I had always seen God as a cosmic 5-0, a cop waiting to haul me in when my warrants matured. I had no idea God was really into fixing messed-up lives. God loves giving people another chance and a new start in life.

I read Ezekiel 16:6-8. It was a story about God taking

care of family, symbolized as a baby that has been abandoned at birth. The baby is thrown out into a field, left to die. Just like Brenda's baby. It is squirming in its blood, writhing and struggling for life. God then passes by the field and says to the baby, "Live!"

God takes the baby home, cares for it, gives it the very best things in life and watches it grow up to become a beautiful adult. When the baby is old enough, God enters into an everlasting covenant and marries the person that was once the baby left to die in the field.

Live! God is in the business of giving life to people who are secretly dying a slow, unnoticed death. I needed that life deep in my empty soul.

As I read God's words to me, my soul caught fire. The image of the baby in the field exactly captured my loneliness, my insecurity and my anger about how life had done me wrong. I wanted God to say "Live!" to me and give me a new life.

That day I felt God had somehow filled the hole in my soul. That was ten years ago. Ten years later, the promise has come true. I've been taken into God's own home. God has brought healing to my family that was torn up. God has given me peace about my past

enty-one-year-old body, this was rest.
enty-one-year-old soul, this was salvation.
enty-one-year-old dreamer, this was a dream

.
enty-one-year-old woman, this is long-
spect and personhood.

od whispered.
he entire world that I love you."

e that . . . a new lover has arrived.
e that . . . this one stays—not just for the
for the days.
e that . . . her innocence is being restored.
e that . . . the dawn finally comes.

t a child.

a's got a hope.

nportant, Brenda's child has got a mother!
oth have a Father.

ther told them both to live!

and all the hurts I have endured and inflicted on
others. I still have my terrible days when I want to stop.
But I gain hope when I remember where I once was.
God loves bringing healing to Brenda. And her babies.
And me. And you. God loves bringing home babies
who are squirming in the field.

God told me to live.

God took me home.

God gave me a whole new life.

God gave me another chance.

God noticed my slow, painful death—and my inability
to do anything about it.

God has hooked me up.

▼

I want to invite everyone to experience this kind of
amazing love . . .

Whether you're like Brenda,
Or whether you're like Brenda's sister who was
irritated by her mood swings,

Or whether you're like Brenda's family who didn't
understand her immaturity,
Or whether you're like Brenda's cousin who violated
her trust, her future and her body,
Or even if you're like Brenda's baby.

You're in need of love—and guess what. God wants
to love you the right way.

Being loved the right way doesn't mean that God will
allow you to avoid all of life's pain.

And it doesn't mean that everything will be perfectly
smooth.

It does mean, however, that God will help you to
recover from what has almost broken you,

Almost destroyed you . . .

And although the pains of yesterday can never fully be
forgotten—nor should they be—your tomorrow can
look like this . . .

THE RESCUE: ENTRANCE OF THE HEALER

A gentle, friendly knock . . . (no response).

The healer stands at the door and continues to knock.

Shhhhh!

Step step step

Tippy-toe . . . tippy-toe .

Shhhhh!

The knob slowly turns . .

c-l-i-c-k

c—r—e—a—k—

The door opens very slo

Not just a door to Brend
But the door to her hea
A door to Brenda's inno
A door to Brenda's drea
A door to Brenda's very
A door to Brenda's adu
childhood.

God did knock,
Again and again and a
And finally
Was invited in.

To this twenty-one-year

relief.
To this tw
To this tw
To this tw
come true
To this tw
overdue r

"Live!" G
"And tell

And just li
And just li
nights but
And just li
And just li

Brenda's g

Now Brend

But most i
And they

And the Fa

▼

I REMEMBER SOME THINGS about high school. Like the first time I met John Blaze. I had never inhaled before, so I was a little nervous. It was lunchtime and we had ten minutes before class started. I had a math test, but I didn't think smoking chronic for the first time would affect me that much. As we started blazing, I saw Jessie, the campus narc, coming toward us. I took my last hit, ducked around the corner and headed off for class. I popped in some Visine and a piece of gum. As I sat down at my desk, I realized I was seriously faded. My mouth was suddenly full of cotton balls. I had the laugh attack going. That was the hardest math test I ever took.

In high school we were looking for adventure. My friends and I wanted to be bad boys, draw the ladies and do it all with style. My best friend was a DJ. It was the mid 1980s and hip-hop was just beginning to take full force. We were living the life at the house parties and the LA clubs. As I hear Tupac rapping about high school, I relate.

> *As I bail through tha empty halls*
>
> *breath stinkin'*
>
> *in my draws*
>
> *ring, ring, ring*
>
> *quiet y'all*
>
> *incoming call*
>
> *plus this my homie from high school*
>
> *he's getting by*
>
> *It's time to bury another brotha nobody cry*
>
> *life as a baller*
>
> *alcohol and booty calls*
>
> *we usta do them as adolescents*
>
> *do you recall?*
>
> *raised as G's*
>
> *loc'ed out and blazed the weed*
>
> *get on tha roof*
>
> *let's get smoked out*
>
> *and blaze with me*

▼

I also relate to Tupac about what it is like to lose friends. Living reckless means you sometimes have to say goodbye early. Real life is full of guns, fights, going before judges, drunk driving accidents and senseless deaths. I know what loss is all about. Burying your friends before they turn eighteen will do terrible things to your soul. It is hard to stay positive when your entire world is negative.

I understand where Tupac is coming from.

But as I listen to his art and look at the broader scope of his life, I hear mixed messages. Tupac really wanted change. But he was so deep in the game, he couldn't really imagine a life that wasn't full of all the negative things that pulled him down. He wanted to change. Or did he?

Yet as I listen to his insightful commentary on issues that many organizations, schools, families and even churches are afraid to touch, I wonder how many times he wanted to change but didn't think it could really be different. How often did Tupac envision himself getting out of the game? How many times did something happen that froze him and made him seriously consider getting out? True spiritual growth is all about listening to the wake-up calls and moving ahead in new directions with Jesus.

I was watching the five o'clock news, and the top story was a freeway shooting in my hometown. The report said that the shooter opened fire on the same freeway I took every single day. Six rounds were blasted into the cab of a truck. Three bullets hit the driver in the leg. He happened to be an off-duty police officer. And despite the burn, he got a real good look at the shooter. They whipped up a sketch and sent it to the news.

That sketch hit me like a ton of bricks. The shooter was one of my best friends. We had been partying together the night he shot the cop. I'd gone home early. If I had stayed that night, I would have been in that car. My friends were involved in a big drug deal. They brought a gun. On the way to the pickup, they were cut off by this truck. They yelled at each other and tried to run each other off the road. Shots were fired. My friend ended up as the top story on the five o'clock news. All three went to youth prison. I heard a wake-up call that day.

I am not naive. I know that change is difficult. People just don't become different people overnight. But we must look at the direction things are going and ask ourselves hard questions. That is what spiritual life is all about: choices. Life will go on. But what life are we choosing? Do we really think spiritual change can happen for us? Or do we resign ourselves to watching life go on for others?

Sometimes we're just like Tupac in this song. We're so given over to death that it occupies all our thoughts and energies. It's hard to enjoy life when death seems like the answer to all life's problems. So we just sit back—paralyzed by life, energized by the thought of death, resigned to the fact that we'll never overcome.

But is this how it's supposed to be?

There was a man who had a special encounter with Jesus in the Bible.

I like to refer to him as Ricky.

Ricky was crippled from birth. Something went wrong in the birthing process, and his legs just never grew properly.

There was a special pond that was called Bethesda,

and sick people would come there because it was said that angels would come and stir the water and the first person in would be completely healed of what was bothering them.

Ricky came to this pool one day,
And sat there,
And sat there,
And sat there,
For thirty-eight years.

Thirty-eight years!!

That's a real long time.

A lot can happen in thirty-eight years:

For example . . .
Thirty-eight years ago, no one knew what a website was.
Or a PC.
A laptop.
A microwave oven.
A calling card.
Hip-hop music.
A DVD.
A VCR.
An SUV.

Cable TV.
HBO.
Sports Center.
A fax.
E-mail.
Digital cameras.
Instant credit.
Instant grits.
Instant replays.
Instant messages.
Rollerblades.
Disposable razors.
Gheri Curls.

Well, you get my point—a lot can happen in thirty-eight years.

That's a long time.
That's a long time to be sick.
That's a long time to just watch others get better.

Just think for a second: people who were infants when Ricky was first carried to the pool were now grandparents!

Meanwhile, life goes on . . .

If not for Ricky, it certainly goes on for the lucky folks

who beat him to the pond.

But one day Jesus shows up, and something about Ricky catches his eye.

(Jesus always notices. No one lives, dies or suffers without his knowledge.)

It probably wasn't his faith.
It probably wasn't his positive attitude.
And it probably wasn't his good deeds.
I am sure it wasn't his winsome personality.

Sometimes our desperation is enough to get the Master's attention.

And Ricky had Jesus' undivided attention.

"Do you even want to get better?" Jesus challenged Ricky.

Shocked that Jesus noticed him—he had felt so invisible and so insignificant for so long.

"I don't have anyone to place me in the pond once it's been stirred by the angels. Once I get to the pool someone has already beaten me to the miracle," replied Ricky, in defense of his own complacency.

And while Ricky was still speaking, Jesus commanded him to stand up and to take his sleeping bag with him.

Ricky did, and was healed on the spot.

"Go your way and stop sinning" were Jesus' parting words to Ricky.

Sinning?

What was Jesus talking about?

I can't picture Ricky sinning a whole lot.

What kind of sinning could Ricky have been involved in?
Where did he go to sin? He sat beside the pool all day . . .
What did he do?
Wouldn't it have been easy to catch him in the act?
Was he a thief?
Was he a pickpocket?
Was he a womanizer?
Was he a pimp?
Did he sell drugs to the other sick people who missed their healing too?

Hmmm . . . I don't know.

But what just happened here? What's the moral of this story?

Is this a story about people being unkind and dissin' crippled folks?

Is this a lesson about not parking in handicap slots?

Is this a moral lesson about helping people who can't walk, talk, hear or see?

Or . . .

Is this a lesson about people who are more lame in their thinking, faith and actions than they are in their bodies?

Could this be the sin that Jesus was referring to?

Could Ricky's sin have been giving up and refusing to live?

Sitting back and hoping for only the worst?

Doubting that life has anything good?

Living as though the very life and breath of God were nonexistent in him?

Or perhaps missing a "divine appointment"—y'know, when a window of opportunity opens to do things differently?

It's that moment when something happens and the prison gates of your mind fling open and you have only a split second to decide whether the energy you'll need to escape is worth the hell you'll pay if caught.

When the opportunity is bigger than you . . .

When you just happen to meet someone special at a place you weren't supposed to be.

When you strike up a casual conversation with someone at a party while you're waiting for a friend and this person becomes your soul mate for life.

When you happen to meet a friend of a friend of a friend, who happens to introduce you to the manager of a company where you've been trying to work for years.

That's a divine appointment. We've all had them.

Like when John saw the sketch of his buddy on the evening news and a small voice within said, "John, this isn't you. Take a detour—get off this road."

Maybe it's a sin to ignore these divine appointments.

To slam the door in the face of divine appointments.

To hang up on the call of fate.

Perhaps this is a parable about what happens when you give up hope and when hope just vanishes from before your eyes.

This happens when people just sit back and watch everyone else live but think it could never happen for them.

Hmmm.

I think the pond in this Bible passage represents opportunity.

Ricky represents hurting humanity.

Jesus represents hope because he is hope. And he offers hope through his words and spirit.

Ricky didn't take advantage of the pool because maybe he felt that his physical status, gender, financial background, credit report, color, prison record, gang affiliation, high school dropout record, poor work record, broken relationships or maybe even his distant or absent father disqualified him from getting into the pool. So he sat watching others enjoying life and grew more and more bitter.

Thirty-eight years of missed opportunities.
Thirty-eight years of pain . . . emotional pain.

But "hope" shows up and is closer and more
refreshing than the pond, actually.

"Hope" has walked up on Ricky and is about to call
Ricky out.

Ha!

The mountain comes to Muhammad!

Hopeless, dreamless Ricky.

And that mountain of hope reaches out to Ricky,
because he doesn't have the strength to reach
out to it.

And Ricky climbs its peak and surveys the valleys
where he once lived, dreamlessly, hopelessly and
angrily . . .

Until Jesus shows up and tells Ricky, "Live!"

Ricky got up and walked away.

And lived.

And life goes on for Ricky.

And it can for you too.

It can even happen for a G.

Yes, even for a G!

Straight up.

Jesus came from a whole line of misfits,
And outlaws.

His great-great-great-grandpa David was a murderer.
He plotted to kill in order to take another man's wife.

And his great-great-great-great Big Mama Rahab was
a prostitute. She rented out her body for a living.

And underneath the shade of Jesus' family tree lies the
rotten fruit of
Rapists
Incestuous relatives
Liars
Cheats
Pimps
Idol worshipers
Sex addicts

Whoa!

Some family, huh?

And Jesus never disowns them.

He doesn't even criticize them.

The Bible even lists their names and sins.

Jesus came to save 'em.

And Jesus even had some Gs in his posse.

Matthew was a straight-up crook. He was Jewish, but he collected taxes for the oppressive Roman government. Tax collectors would often add their own "tax" on top of what the Romans required. It was one thing for the Romans to rob the Jewish people; but it was wrong for Matthew to pimp his own people.

When the Bible wants to show examples of the worst of the worst sinners, tax collectors are used.

But Matthew came to work for Jesus. And Jesus respected him, loved him and saved him.

Simon the Zealot was a Jewish nationalist. He wanted to see the oppression of the Roman Empire come to an end. We got our English word *zeal* from the name Zealot, because they were passionate about their freedom. Simon was considered an outlaw by the Roman government. Similar to the way our government might view a Black Panther member. To the Roman government, this man was a potential guerrilla warfare soldier.

But Simon came to work for Jesus. And Jesus respected him, loved him and saved him.

And by now everyone knows that Judas was a crook.

He kept Jesus' books and managed his finances. And Jesus respected him and loved him. But Judas didn't think he could be saved from his crimes—so he took his own life and hanged himself because of tremendous pain and guilt.

Is there a heaven for a G?

You bet!

But that G has to leave his old comfortable place, what's familiar, and pick up his sleeping bag to follow Jesus.

> *Jesus said to her, "I am the resurrection and the life. He who believes in me will live, even though he dies." (John 11:25)*

You gotta **follow** Jesus.

Then life will go on!

And so will we . . .

A LOT OF RELIGIOUS PEOPLE TALK ABOUT something called repentance. Unfortunately, we have misunderstood the word.

To repent does not mean to be sorry. To repent means to be changed. It literally means to have a paradigm shift. In other words, it is seeing things from a different perspective, in a totally new way.

For example, when we were kids and saw two adults kissing, we thought it was the nastiest thing ever.

Then adolescence hit!

We don't see it as nasty anymore. We like it. We like it a lot.

Our paradigm has shifted. We have repented of the notion that kissing is gross.

God is calling us to be a part of the divine family—and it's not as hard as many think. God isn't asking us to be perfect but to be willing to be changed by divine love.

And changed by God's Word.

▼

Tupac cries out for a new day in his song "Changes."
He believed that if you take the evil out of people they
will act right.

> *We gotta make a change . . .*
>
> *It's time for us as a people to start
> makin' some changes.*
>
> *Let's change the way we eat,
> let's change the way we live*
>
> *and let's change the way we
> treat each other.*
>
> *You see the old way wasn't working
> so it's on us to do*
>
> *what we gotta do, to survive.*

But you can't just take evil out of people without
replacing it with something else. Evil provides energy
for evil people; it motivates much of what they do. If
that evil is to be removed, it needs to be replaced with
something that is equally powerful and equally

motivating . . . like love.

Love is a funny thing. It isn't soft and fuzzy. It's more than cute and cuddly. It isn't just celebrated on St. Valentine's Day. And it isn't merely an emotion.

Love will turn otherwise passive men into Ridahs.

Love has assisted frail mothers in crisis who need to lift an automobile off their child.

Love makes a horrified parent run into a burning building to rescue a child.

Love makes a man go legit so that he can be with his family.

And love makes a single mother work three jobs to make sure her children can have a good education and music lessons.

This kind of love is a gift from God. This kind of love will absolutely change you.

You see, we can't really change our world. I can't even make my six-year-old eat her vegetables consistently. I can't stop my beard from graying. And I can't make people happy. Why would I think I could change the whole world?

But . . .

Love has transformed me so that my paradigm is shifted . . . and I see the world so much differently. I can now see
Strength in my weaknesses,
Insight in my struggles,
Lofty attributes in lowly things,
Lessons in failures,
Faith in my fear.
Good in bad situations.
Good in my graying beard.
And good in others who are different from me.

This kind of love is available to everyone—anyone.

God longs to demonstrate that love through the Son. Jesus longs for us to see each as brothers/sisters and not as two distant strangers (to quote Tupac).

What does this mean?

It means that God is tired of having us think of him as a bustah! God is not the end of fun but the Fountain of Life. God is the inventor of fun and recreation. God doesn't want to be your enemy. And God gets no joy when we choose to be his.

One of the lines of "Changes" says, "I'd love to go back to where we played as kids—but things change and that's the way it is." Tupac is longing for the simplicity of the old days.

We trusted back then.
We loved back then.
We were carefree back then.

But something happened that made us change.

But thanks to God, we can change again.

▼

Here's what you need to know about Jesus:
He was hardcore!

He loved hard!
He lived hard!
He preached hard!
He died hard!

He was God's Lamb—which is just another way of saying that he let himself become our scapegoat! The one who would be blamed for our screw-ups so that we'd come up smelling like roses to God.

Jesus is relevant and can relate to people who are hurting.

You can tell a whole lot about a person by the way they treat outsiders.

Jesus was not concerned with his reputation, so he wasn't ashamed to kick it with the outcasts of society. He was often treated as an outcast. That is why he was comfortable hanging out with people who were disliked and disrespected—this is who he came to rescue.

He hung out with hos and showed them respect—and was criticized for it.

He hung out with tax collectors (Matthew 9:10; 10:3), who were on the same level as today's drug dealers who sell to children in their own neighborhoods.

He hung out with the Zealots, the Jewish nationalists (Luke 6:15). These would be the folks who have FBI files today.

He touched the lepers (Luke 17; Mark 5), who were like our AIDS victims. Remember when the world ooohhh'd and aaahhhh'd when Princess Diana visited and touched people who were dying of AIDS? It took the world's breath away that royalty would stoop so low. Jesus set the precedent for this two thousand years ago.

Jesus made time for children (Mark 10) and saw them as important.

Jesus spent time with the homeless and mentally ill (Mark 5).

Jesus wasn't a typical kind of preacher! Or rabbi, as it was called in his day. Jesus obviously cared about the injustices of his day. He was concerned about all the wrong he saw. And Jesus is concerned about the people who are hurting today. That is precisely why he is calling us to lead his charge to make the world a better and safer place to live. Jesus put the desire for change in Tupac's heart. Jesus is change. The only constant in life is change.

▼

And as long as I stay black,
I gotta stay strapped,

And I never get to lay back

'Cause I always gotta worry

> *'bout the paybacks*
>
> *Some buck that I roughed up way back*
>
> *Comin' back after all these years*
>
> *Rat-a-tat-tat-tat-tat. That's the way it is.*

We want you to know what God thinks about Gs and about what's happening down here.

The way Jesus was murdered was considered to be severe, execution-style. This was the kind of death that was reserved for outlaws and slaves. It was the cruelest form of execution practiced in the Roman Empire. The guilty were usually stripped and beaten with leather thongs with pieces of bone in the ends. This was done to weaken them before forcing them to carry their cross and parade in total humiliation before their judges and their own families. The idea was to discourage anyone from considering similar crimes. The criminal was then stripped naked and nailed to the cross. They were left there to die of hunger and exhaustion.

Jesus wasn't some soft fake-smile-wearin' evangelist who wanted riches, fame and a ministry named after himself. He was what Tupac and his crew would call a Ridah. He knew full well what he was riding into, and he never strayed from the path. Because he knew this was the only way for a G to get to heaven.

Jesus knows what we struggle with.
Racism,
Sexism,
Discrimination in housing, education and employment.
Hunger,
Disproportionate numbers of African Americans in prison,
Glass ceilings,
Negative images in the media,
And a society that for the most part doesn't believe that these issues even exist today.
Therefore they choose to be a part of the problem and not the solution. Then everyone pays!

Sigh!

God wants this generation to know that he ain't mad atcha. He has mad love for his creation and wants to make us family.

Finally, Jesus was crucified between two thieves. Although one of them tried to make fun of Jesus, the other one asked Jesus to remember him in heaven.

This convicted G realized that Jesus was different, not the average G. Jesus, touched by this man's faith, replied, "Today you will be with me in paradise."

Remember, Jesus was considered to be a G.

The government conspired to kill him shortly after birth.

He was a refugee in Africa.

He came back home and lost his life on a cross—executed just like a G.

And all of this was done so that the Father could say "I ain't mad atcha" and make us his children.

So is there a heaven for a G?

You know this . . .

But it's only through siding up with a Ridah named Jesus.

And following him.

And going a new way.

That is repentance.

Repentance is the key to change.

Jesus said to them, "I tell you the truth, the tax collectors and the prostitutes are entering the kingdom of God ahead of you. For John came to you to show you the way of righteousness, and you did not believe him, but the tax collectors and the prostitutes did. And even after you saw this, you did not repent and believe him. (Matthew 21:31-32)

MY FIRST MEMORY OF BASKETBALL is the night Magic Johnson was a rookie and scored forty-two points to win his first NBA title.

Because of my love for the Lakers and good leadership, I am also a huge Phil Jackson fan. Before Phil came to Los Angeles, the Shaq and Kobe Lakers had exactly zero titles. They lacked team chemistry, and they weren't challenged to be the best basketball players they could become. Phil came with a new system, and in his first year the Lakers became the world champions. Shaquille O'Neal became the most valuable player of the NBA. The Lakers and Phil have gone on to win three titles in a row, with more on the horizon.

Where would the Lakers be without Phil and his leadership? Where would the Lakers be without his new system that focuses on team first, defense and respect for the game? No playa is larger than the game. The Lakers believed in Phil and his system, and he led them to the bling bling of title rings.

▼

Jesus wants to lead you to spiritual and emotional victory in your life. You have seen the stars in the sky. You have heard the beats. You have seen what God is like through the seven songs from Tupac and Lauryn. You may be in the same situation spiritually that the Lakers were when Phil first came on the scene. Shaq and Kobe had heard a lot about him. They knew he was successful because his system had worked in Chicago. But they weren't sure whether they would trust him. Would his leadership really get them NBA ice? Would they trust him? Would they follow his lead? That's what faith is all about.

In the same way, you have probably heard some things about Jesus. You know that he is all about love and brings good things to people's lives. But now you have heard from him in a new way. He has spoken to you. He has called you into his office. He wants you to join his team. Will you trust him? Will you let him be your leader? If you do, he promises that his leadership will get you to the real promised land. He does not promise an NBA banner and ring. He promises eternal life, today and forever!

> *"There was a man who had two sons. He went to the first and said, 'Son, go work today in the vineyard.'*
>
> *" 'I will not,' he answered, but later he changed his mind and went.*
>
> *"Then the father went to the other son and said the same thing. He answered, 'I will sir,' but he did not go.*
>
> *"Which of the two did what his father wanted?"*
>
> *"The first," they answered.*
>
> *Jesus said to them, "I tell you the truth, the tax collectors and the prostitutes are entering the kingdom of God ahead of you." (Matthew 21:28-31)*

Spiritual growth is not rocket science. One of the reasons so many of us find it hard to become the people God made us to become is that we make it more complex than it really is. Jesus tells us how to grow. The key is to *do* the will of the Father. It isn't how eloquent or impressive our religious language is. God really doesn't care. The second son sounded like a great guy. He even called his dad sir. The first son sounded like a bustah and dissed his dad. But he woke up, smelled the coffee and went to work. He did the will of the father. If you want to grow spiritually, the key is to do God's will. Don't talk about it. Be about it. Then you will know Jesus and be part of his family in this world.

Faith is obeying leadership. The Lakers showed basketball faith by obeying Phil Jackson. He told them to run the triangle offense. They learned to pass. He called them to better conditioning. They ran, lifted weights and ate better. He called them to become friends. They cooled out together and became more than acquaintances. They had faith.

In the same way, Jesus is calling us to faith in him and his leadership. He has a plan for how we should live. He wants us to get into spiritual shape. He is deeply concerned about and committed to our relationships. The question is whether we will do what he says. When he calls us to challenges and things we don't like, will we have faith and obey Jesus, or will we go prima donna, think we know what is better and lose the championship? Will we let Jesus be our leader?

As we see the stars and listen to the beats, we follow the Living God who has been pursued for generations. We will not be disappointed. Our faith will be rewarded.

Stay up and stay strong in God!

Much love,
Alex Gee and John Teter

I appreciate you, Jesus, for loving me, enjoying me and believing in me.

Jackie and Lexi, my wife and daughter and the loves of my life. Thank you for giving me space to write this book.

Thank you mom (Verline) for teaching me how to read and write (smile).

Thanks to my brother (Edward) for your friendship and to my sister and muse (Lilada) for reminding me that I am a writer.

F.O.L. Church: You make me want to be a better pastor.

My grown "kids": Marcus, Shadrina and Nicole.

My armor bearers, my Thursday morning crew and my hip-hop historians (Roberto, Marlon, Arthur and Ant): You men all inspire me.

Mad respect for friends like Steve Hayner, Ken Gire

and Parker Palmer, who convinced me that I have writing talent.

Mad love for the manager at Perkins on the West Beltline (Madison) who let us write there even after closing.

Cindy Bunch, our pushy white editor (smile), who appreciated our voice.

The positive hip-hop artists who attempt to raise our awareness about key issues in society.

▼

Becky, thank you for being the best. You make my life rich with joy and laughter.

Mom, thank you for teaching me music and how to cross cultures.

George Teter, much love for scoring me Lauryn Hill tickets in 1999. A seed was planted.

Chris Getz, you exposed me to Def Jam and taught me, "Don't believe the hype!"

D. H. More Than Conquerors, thank you for walking in the truth. You bring me joy.

Dorian Stephens, much respect for caring about the DH hip-hop community. Julie Chan, big ups for regulating all things on the web. Your gifts are appreciated.

Barnes and Noble, Manhattan Beach, thanks for going above and beyond.

Andy Le Peau, Cindy Bunch and Greg Vigne, thanks for the meeting in Madison. Who knew?

Alex Gee is pastor of Fountain of
Life Family Worship Center and
president and founder of the
Nehemiah Community Development Corporation, both in
Madison, Wisconsin. He also
founded and owns AGAPPE, an executive coaching
and consulting company. To contact Alex, send an
e-mail to <alex@alexgee.com>. You can also visit his
website at <www.alexgee.com>.

John Teter serves InterVarsity
Christian Fellowship/USA as area
director for Metro South LA. He is
also the author of *Get the Word
Out.* To contact John, e-mail
<getthewordout@charter.net>.
You can also go to his website at
<www.gtwoministries.com>.

Both Alex and John are available for conference

speaking and evangelism training. E-mail them for more information.

Visit the *Jesus & the Hip-Hop Prophets* website at <www.hiphopprophets.com>.